# Hindu
## Mandir

*For Mishka, Lasya, and Tula Nansi*

For a free color catalog describing Gareth Stevens' list of high-quality books and multimedia programs, call 1-800-542-2595 (USA) or 1-800-461-9120 (Canada). Gareth Stevens Publishing's Fax: (414) 225-0377.

Gareth Stevens Publishing thanks Shrinivas G. Joshi, Ph.D., for his assistance with the accuracy of the text. Dr. Joshi is a native of India and received academic degrees from the University of Poona and the Indian Institute of Science-Bangalore, as well as from the University of California-Berkeley. He is currently a Professor of Electrical and Computer Engineering at Marquette University, Milwaukee, Wisconsin. He is also president of the India Music Society in Milwaukee.

Library of Congress Cataloging-in-Publication Data available upon request from publisher. Fax: (414) 225-0377 for the attention of the Publishing Records Department.

ISBN 0-8368-2607-8

This North American edition first published in 2000 by
**Gareth Stevens Publishing**
1555 North RiverCenter Drive, Suite 201
Milwaukee, WI 53212 USA

Original edition © 1998 by Franklin Watts.
First published in 1998 by Franklin Watts,
96 Leonard Street, London EC2A 4RH, England.
This U. S. edition © 2000 by Gareth Stevens, Inc.
Additional end matter © 2000 by Gareth Stevens, Inc.

Editor: Samantha Armstrong
Series Designer: Kirstie Billingham
Illustrator: Gemini Patel
Religious Education Consultant: Margaret Barratt, Religious Education Teacher Advisor
Religious Advisors: Shree Vishwa Mandir, Southall
Reading Consultant: Prue Goodwin, Reading and Language Information Centre, Reading

Gareth Stevens Series Editor: Dorothy L. Gibbs

Photographic acknowledgements:
Cover: Steve Shott Photography.
Inside: p. 6 Sonia Halliday Photography; p. 7 (top) Circa; p. 22 (right) Trip Photographic Library.
All other photographs by Steve Shott Photography.

With thanks to the Shree Vishwa Mandir, Southall; the Bhaktivedanta Manor, Hertfordshire; and Suriacumar, Rekha, and Khiloni Meggi.

Printed in the United States of America

1 2 3 4 5 6 7 8 9 04 03 02 01 00

# PLACES OF WORSHIP

# Hindu
# Mandir

Angela Wood

Gareth Stevens Publishing
**MILWAUKEE**

Om, or aum, is a symbol used
to represent the Hindu faith.

# Contents

Words that appear in the glossary are printed in **boldface**
type the first time they occur in the text.

# Mandirs around the World

A **mandir** is a place where Hindus meet to **worship**. It can be a large building or a small **shrine** in a home. There are mandirs all around the world.

◀ This mandir is in India.

# Hindu Beliefs

Most Hindu people worship in their homes. The Hindu word for "worship" is *puja*.

▼ Each of these statues, or murtis, shows a different god.

Hindus believe in many gods. They say that God can be seen in a person or in an animal. Inside a mandir are statues or pictures called **murtis**. Each murti shows a god that is different from any other.

# Going to a Mandir

When Hindus visit a mandir, they always take off their shoes and leave them outside to show their **respect** for the murtis.

When Hindus enter the mandir, the first thing they do is ring a bell. Ringing the bell is like knocking at the door. It lets someone know that a person is there.

# Making an Offering

Many Hindus have a murti that is special to them at the mandir. They show their love for that god by offering it something, such as water, food, **incense**, or a lit candle.

▲ Sometimes Hindus put a money offering in a collection box.

This woman is pouring milk ▶ over a murti as an offering.

# Ganesh

Most mandirs have a murti of the god **Ganesh**.
Ganesh has a man's body with an elephant's head.
Hindus worship Ganesh when they begin their
prayers or start something new.

◀ The tiny mouse at
Ganesh's feet is not
afraid. Although
Ganesh is big, he is
very gentle, and he
brings good luck.
Hindus have offered
coins to this murti
of Ganesh.

# Vishnu

This murti is of the god **Vishnu**. He takes many different animal and human forms. Vishnu protects everyone and everything in the world.

# Krishna and Radha

Vishnu sometimes takes the form of **Krishna**. One story of Krishna says he played his flute for **gopis**, the young women who looked after cows. Krishna was always kind to cows, and he could find them when they got lost.

Hindus think cows are especially good animals. They respect cows for producing enough milk for everyone, not just for their own calves.

◀ Krishna is usually shown with his flute. He played his flute for cows and for the gopis who took care of them.

Krishna's favorite gopi ▶ is his partner, **Radha**.

12

# Rama, Sita, Lakshman,

Many mandirs have a murti of Vishnu as **Rama**. His selfish stepmother made Rama and his wife, Sita, go away from their kingdom for a long time. Rama's younger brother Lakshman went with them. On their travels, a **demon** called Ravana kidnapped Sita. The monkey god Hanuman helped Rama save Sita.

The murti in the middle ▶ is Rama. Sita is on the right, and Lakshman is on the left. Hanuman is in front of Lakshman, worshiping Rama and Sita. Rama and Lakshman always carry bows and arrows so they will be ready to fight off evil.

# and Hanuman

Hanuman was a true friend to Rama, Sita, and Lakshman.

◄ This painting of Ravana, the ten-headed demon, was made by children in a Hindu school.

This murti is of ► the monkey god Hanuman.

15

# Shiva

**Shiva** destroys bad things, such as wars and diseases. He is also known as the Lord of Time and has three eyes so he can look at the past, the present, and the future. Shiva's three-pronged spear shows that he is defeating evil.

Shiva has a river flowing through his hair. ▶
Hindus say it is the Ganges River, which flows through India. They believe this sacred river of life flows from heaven, through Shiva's hair, to Earth.

# A School at the Mandir

Some mandirs have a school where children learn Hindu stories and how to live a Hindu life. They work and play at the school with other Hindu children.

Like most Hindu women, this teacher wears a **sari** with a short blouse. A sari is a long, straight piece of cloth.

To put on a sari, a Hindu woman wraps one end of the cloth around her waist, makes some pleats at the front, and tucks them in. Then she brings the other end of the cloth over her shoulder.

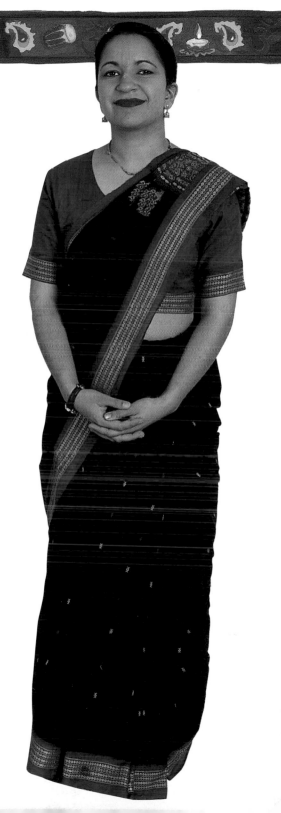

# Showing Respect

When Hindus visit a mandir, they show respect to a murti by putting their hands together in front of their chests and saying the word *Namaste*. *Namaste* means "honor to you."

Hindus often greet a person the same way. Because they believe that God is in everybody, they greet God in everyone they meet.

When Hindus pray in the mandir, they bow.
Sometimes their foreheads touch the floor.
Bowing shows their love and respect for God.

# Dancing in a Mandir

▲ This murti shows Mahadevi as **Durga**, who is a strong, energetic woman.

Hindus often worship by dancing. In the dance, their hands and bodies tell a story.

During Navaratri, the dancing goes on for ▶ nine nights. Navaratri is a festival that honors Mahadevi, or the Great Mother.

22

# Arti

Every day at the mandir, there is a ceremony called **arti**. One person moves an arti lamp in front of a murti. Then, while everyone sings and prays, people in the mandir pass their hands over the lamp's flame and over their foreheads and hair.

Because the arti lamp has been in front of the murti, the people feel they have a blessing from God.

An arti lamp has five flames, one ▶ flame for each of the five senses. The five flames also stand for air, earth, fire, water, and space.

# Music in a Mandir

Worship in a mandir usually includes music. Hindu people play instruments that come from India, such as bells, drums, and tambourines. They also sing together.

Some songs last a long time. They are poems, set to music, that tell stories of God. With bells and drums beating the rhythm, it is easy to join in and clap along with the music.

Sometimes Hindu people **chant**. Chanting is singing in a special way, by repeating a few sounds and words over and over.

# Prasad

As Hindus leave the mandir, they are given **prasad**. Prasad is food that has been offered to God. It is usually sweets, nuts, or fruit.

This **pandit**, or priest, is giving ▶ water and prasad to people as they leave the mandir.

# Glossary

**arti** (<u>art</u>-ee): a daily Hindu ceremony during which people are blessed by God using a lamp with five flames.

**chant:** to sing in a special way, repeating a few words and sounds over and over.

**demon:** an evil spirit.

**Durga** (<u>Door</u>-gah): a god in the form of a strong and powerful woman.

**Ganesh** (Geh-<u>naysh</u>): a god in the form of a man with an elephant's head, who brings good luck.

**gopis** (<u>goh</u>-pees): young women who take care of cows.

**incense:** material that makes sweet-smelling smoke when it is burned.

**Krishna** (<u>Kreesh</u>-nah): the god Vishnu in the form of a baby, a child, or a young man.

**mandir:** a place where Hindus meet to worship.

**murtis** (<u>mer</u>-tees): statues or pictures through which Hindus worship their gods.

**pandit** (<u>pan</u>-det): a Hindu wise man or priest.

**prasad** (prah-<u>sod</u>): blessed food that has been offered to the gods then shared with everyone visiting the mandir.

**puja** (<u>poo</u>-jah): the Hindu word for "worship" or the main form of Hindu worship.

**Radha** (<u>Rahd</u>-ah): a gopi who was Krishna's female partner.

**Rama** (<u>Rah</u>-mah): the god Vishnu in the form of a young prince.

**respect:** to treat with honor and thoughtful consideration.

**sari** (<u>sahr</u>-ee): a long, straight piece of cloth that is wrapped around and worn as a skirt by Hindu women.

**Shiva** (<u>Shiv</u>-ah): the Hindu god who destroys evil things; also known as the Lord of Time.

**shrine:** a place used for religious worship that has a holy or blessed object or image, such as a statue or a picture, as its central point.

**Vishnu** (<u>Vish</u>-noo): the Hindu god who protects everyone and everything in the world.

**worship:** to show love and respect with prayer, usually as part of a religious service.

# More Books to Read

The Broken Tusk: Stories of the Hindu God Ganesha. Uma Krishnaswami (Linnet Books)

The Butter Thief. Chris Murray (Bhaktivedanta Book Trust)

Diwali: Hindu Festival of Lights. Best Holiday Books (series). Dianne M. McMillan (Enslow)

Hindu Festivals. Celebrate (series). Dilip Kadodwala and Paul Gateshill (Heinemann Educational Books)

Holi. World of Holidays (series). Dilip Kadodwala (Raintree/Steck-Vaughn)

India. Festivals of the World (series). Falaq Kagda (Gareth Stevens)

Our Most Dear Friend: Bhagavad-gita for Children. Vishaka Badger and Jean Griesser (Torchlight)

Sacred Myths: Stories of World Religions. Marilyn McFarlane (Sibyl Publications)

What Do We Know About Hinduism? What Do We Know About...? (series). Anita Ganeri (Peter Bedrick Books)

Worlds of Belief: Religion and Spirituality. Our Human Family (series). Lisa Sita (Blackbirch)

# Videos

*Hinduism and the Song of God:  A Modern Interpretation of the Bhagavad Gita.* (Hartley Film Foundation)

*Hinduism:  The Elephant God.* (Films for the Humanities and Sciences)

*How Do You Spell God?* (HBO Kids Video)

# Web Sites

Colors of India
*www.colorsofindia.com*

Daily Life in Ancient India
*members.aol.com/ Donnclass/Indialife.html*

Hindu Kids Universe
*www.hindukids.org*

Hinduism for Schools
*www.btinternet.com/ ~vivekananda/ schools1.htm*

Valmiki's Ramayana
*www.askasia.org/adult_ free_zone/virtual_gallery/ exhibitions/index.htm*

To find additional web sites, use a reliable search engine with one or more of the following keywords: *arti, Ganesh, gopi, Hindu, Hinduism, Krishna, mandir, murti, pandit, puja, Rama, sari, Shiva,* and *Vishnu.*

# Index